The Curious Incident of the Dog in the Night-Time

Abridged for Schools

Adapted from the novel by Mark Haddon

methuen | drama

LONDON • NEW YORK • OXFORD • NEW DELHI • SYDNEY

METHUEN DRAMA
Bloomsbury Publishing Plc
50 Bedford Square, London, WC1B 3DP, UK
1385 Broadway, New York, NY 10018, USA

BLOOMSBURY, METHUEN DRAMA and the Methuen Drama logo are trademarks of
Bloomsbury Publishing Plc

The Curious Incident of the Dog in the Night-Time by Mark Haddon
Adapted for the stage by Simon Stephens

The Curious Incident of the Dog in the Night-Time
was first published in 2003 by Jonathan Cape

Stage adaptation first published in Great Britain by Methuen Drama 2012
This edition first published 2019

Copyright © Cursing and Sobbing Limited and Mark Haddon, 2012, 2019

Simon Stephens has asserted his right under the Copyright, Designs and Patents Act,
1988, to be identified as author of this work.

Series design by Louise Dugdale

A catalogue record for this book is available from the British Library.

A catalog record for this book is available from the Library of Congress.

ISBN: PB: 978-1-3501-1153-0
       ePDF: 978-1-3501-1154-7
       eBook: 978-1-3501-1155-4

Series: Plays for Young People

Typeset by RefineCatch Limited, Bungay, Suffolk

To find out more about our authors and books visit www.bloomsbury.com
and sign up for our newsletters.

The Curious Incident of the
Dog in the Night-Time

Characters

Christopher
Siobhan
Ed
Judy
Mrs Alexander / Voice Two / Posh Woman / Voice Five /
Voice Six
Roger (Mr Shears) / Voice One / Duty Sergeant /
Mr Thompson / Man Behind Counter / Voice Four /
Drunk One
Mrs Shears / Mrs Gascoyne / Woman on Train / Information /
London Policewoman
Reverend Peters / Uncle Terry / Station Policeman / Policeman
One / Mr Wise / Voice Three / Drunk Two

All actors remain on stage unless prescribed otherwise.

There is also a dead dog. With a fork sticking out of it.

Scenes run into one another without interruption regardless of alterations in space or time or chronology.

Scene One   Garden

A dead dog lies in the middle of the stage. A large garden fork is sticking out of its side.

Christopher Boone, *fifteen years old, stands on one side of it. His forty-two-year-old neighbour* **Mrs Shears** *stands on the other.*

They stand for a while without saying anything. The rest of the company watch, waiting to see who is going to dare to speak first.

Mrs Shears   Holy fuck. What have you done?

Christopher *is frozen to the spot.*

Mrs Shears   Oh no. Oh fuck no.

Christopher's *teacher* **Siobhan** *opens* **Christopher**'s *book. She reads from it.*

Siobhan   It was seven minutes after midnight. The dog was lying on the grass in the middle of the lawn in front of Mrs Shears's house.

Its eyes were closed. It looked as if it was running on its side, the way dogs run when they think they are chasing a cat in a dream. But the dog was not running or asleep. The dog was dead.

Mrs Shears   Get away from my dog.

Siobhan   There was a garden fork sticking out of the dog. The dog was called Wellington. It belonged to Mrs Shears who was our friend. She lived on the opposite side of the road, two houses to the left.

Mrs Shears   Get away from my dog.

Christopher *takes two steps away from the dog.*

Siobhan   My name is Christopher John Francis Boone. I live at 36 Randolph Street, Swindon, Wiltshire. I know all the countries of the world and capital cities. And every prime number up to 7507.

Mrs Shears   Get away from my dog for Christ's sake.

Christopher *puts his hands over his ears. He closes his eyes. He rolls forward. He presses his forehead onto the grass. He starts groaning.*

Siobhan   After twelve and a half minutes a policeman arrived. He had a big orange leaf stuck to the bottom of his shoe which was poking out from one side. This is good, Christopher. It's quite exciting. I like the details. They make it more realistic.

A **Policeman** *enters. He has a big orange leaf stuck to the bottom of his shoe, which is poking out to one side. He squats next to* **Christopher**.

Siobhan   He squatted down next to me. He said to me:

Christopher *stops groaning.*

Policeman One   Would you like to tell me what's going on here, young man?

Christopher *lifts his head from the ground.*

There is some time.

Christopher *looks at the* **Policeman**.

There is some time.

Siobhan   I do not tell lies. Mother used to say that this was because I was a good person. But it is not because I am a good person. It is because I can't tell lies.

Christopher   The dog is dead.

Policeman One   I'd got that far.

Christopher   I think someone killed the dog.

Policeman One   How old are you?

Christopher   I'm fifteen years and three months and two days.

Policeman One   And what precisely are you doing in the garden?

Christopher   I'm talking to you.

Policeman One   OK, why were you in the garden in the first place?

Christopher   I was holding the dog.

Policeman One   Why were you holding the dog?

Christopher   I like dogs.

Policeman One   Did you kill the dog?

Christopher   I did not kill the dog.

Policeman One   You seem very upset about this.

I'm going to ask you once again.

Christopher *starts groaning.*

Policeman One   Terrific.

Christopher *carries on groaning.*

Policeman One   Young man I'm going to ask you to stop making that noise and to stand up please calmly and quietly.

Christopher *carries on groaning.*

Policeman One   Marvellous. Great. Just flipping –

The **Policeman** *tries to lift him up by his arm.*

Christopher *screams. He hits the* **Policeman***.*

The **Policeman** *stares at* **Christopher***. For a while the two look at one another, neither entirely sure what to say or quite believing what has just happened.*

Policeman One   I'm arresting you for assaulting a police officer.

I strongly advise you to get into the back of the police car because if you try any of that monkey business again, you little shit, I am going to seriously lose my rag. Is that understood?

Scene Two   School

Siobhan   I find people confusing. This is for two main reasons. The first main reason is that people do a lot of talking without using any words. Siobhan says that if you raise one eyebrow it can mean lots of different things. It can mean, 'I want to do sex with you.' I never said that.

Christopher   Yes you did.

Siobhan   I didn't use those words, Christopher.

Christopher   You did on September 12th last year. At first break.

Siobhan   And it can also mean 'I think that what you just said was very stupid.'

Scene Three   Police Station

Duty Sergeant   Could you empty your pockets onto the desk please, Christopher?

Christopher   Is that in case I have anything in them that I could use to kill myself or escape or attack a policeman with.

The **Duty Sergeant** *looks at him for a beat.*

Duty Sergeant   That's right.

Christopher   I've got a Swiss Army knife but I only use that for doing 'odd jobs' not for stabbing things or hurting people.

Duty Sergeant   Jolly good.

Christopher *empties his pockets.*

Voice Three   A piece of string.

Voice One   A piece of a wooden puzzle.

Voice Six   Three pellets of rat food for Toby, my pet rat.

Voice Three   £1.47 (made up of a £1 coin, a 20p coin, two 10p coins, a 5p coin and a 2p coin).

Voice Six   A red paperclip.

Voice Three   A key for the front door.

Voice One   A Swiss Army knife with thirteen attachments including a wire stripper and a saw and a toothpick and tweezers.

Duty Sergeant   Could you take your watch off please, Christopher?

Christopher   No.

Duty Sergeant   I'm sorry, Christopher?

Christopher   I need my watch to know exactly what time it is.

Duty Sergeant   Give it here, lad.

Christopher *screams.*

Duty Sergeant   All right, son, you keep it. Do you have any family, Christopher?

Christopher   Yes I do.

Duty Sergeant   And who is your family?

Christopher   Father and Mother but Mother is dead. And also Uncle Terry who is in Sunderland. He is my father's brother. And my grandparents too but three of them are dead and Grandma Burton lives in a home because she has senile dementia and thinks I'm someone on television.

Duty Sergeant   Right. Lovely. Do you know your father's phone number, Christopher?

Scene Four   Police Station

Christopher *turns to* **Ed.** **Ed** *looks at him. He holds his hand out in front of him with his fingers stretched.* **Christopher** *does the same. They touch fingers. Then let go.*

Duty Sergeant   Christopher. Mr Boone. Could you come this way please?

I've spoken to your father and he says you didn't mean to hit the policeman. Did you mean to hit the policeman?

Christopher Yes.

Duty Sergeant But you didn't mean to hurt the policeman?

Christopher No. I didn't mean to hurt the policeman, I just wanted him to stop touching me.

Duty Sergeant You do know that it's wrong to hit a policeman don't you?

Christopher I do.

Duty Sergeant Did you kill the dog, Christopher?

Christopher I did not kill the dog.

Duty Sergeant Do you know that it is wrong to lie to a policeman and that you can get into a very great deal of trouble if you do?

Christopher Yes.

Duty Sergeant Do you know who killed the dog?

Christopher No.

Duty Sergeant Are you telling the truth?

Christopher Yes. I always tell the truth.

Duty Sergeant Right. I'm going to give you a caution.

Christopher Is that going to be on a piece of paper like a certificate I can keep?

Duty Sergeant No. A caution means that we are going to keep a record of what you did, that you hit a policeman but that it was an accident and that you didn't mean to hurt the policeman.

Christopher But it wasn't an accident.

Ed Christopher, please.

Duty Sergeant If you get into any more trouble we will take out this record and see that you have been given a caution and we will take things much more seriously. Do you understand what I'm saying?

Christopher   Yes.

Scene Five   School

Siobhan   The second main reason I find people confusing is that people often talk using metaphors. These are examples of metaphors.

Voice Three   I am going to seriously lose my rag.

Voice Six   He was the apple of her eye.

Voice Three   They had a skeleton in the cupboard.

Voice One   We had a real pig of a day.

Voice Two   The dog was stone dead.

Siobhan   The word metaphor means carrying something from one place to another and it is when you describe something by using a word for something that it isn't. This means that the word metaphor is a metaphor. Wow. That's clever.

Christopher   It's true.

Siobhan   Yes. I think it should be called a lie because a pig is not like a day and people do not have skeletons in their cupboards. And when I try and make a picture of the phrase in my head it just confuses me because imagining an apple in someone's eye doesn't have anything to do with liking someone a lot and it makes you forget what the person was talking about.

Scene Six   Home

Christopher *turns to* **Ed**.

Christopher   I'm sorry.

Ed   It's OK.

Christopher   I didn't kill Wellington.

Ed   I know.

Christopher, you have to stay out of trouble, OK?

Christopher   I didn't know I was going to get into trouble. I like Wellington and I went to say hello to him, but I didn't know that someone had killed him.

Ed   Just try and keep your nose out of other people's business.

Christopher   I am going to find out who killed Wellington.

Ed   Were you listening to what I was saying, Christopher?

Christopher   Yes, I was listening to what you were saying but when someone gets murdered you have to find out who did it so that they can be punished.

Ed   It's a bloody dog, Christopher, a bloody dog.

Christopher   I think dogs are important too. I think some dogs are cleverer than some people. Steve, for example, who comes to school on Thursdays, needs help eating his food and he probably couldn't even fetch a stick.

Ed   Leave it.

Christopher   I wonder if the police will find out who killed him and punish the person.

Ed   I said leave it, for God's sake.

Christopher   Are you sad about Wellington?

Ed   Yes, Christopher, you could say that. You could very well say that.

Siobhan *reads more from the book.*

Scene Seven   Home

Siobhan   Mother died two years ago.

I came home from school one day and no one answered the door, so I went and found the secret key that we keep under a flowerpot outside the kitchen window. I let myself into the house and wiped my feet on the mat. I put the key in the bowl on the table. I took my coat off and hung it by the side of the fridge so it would be ready for school the next day and gave three pellets of rat food to Toby who is my pet rat. I made myself a raspberry milkshake and heated it up in the microwave. Then I went up to my bedroom and turned on my bedroom light and played six games of Tetris and got to level 38 which is my fourth best ever score.

He was away for two and a half hours. When he came back I went downstairs.

Ed   I'm afraid you won't be seeing your mother for a while.

Christopher   Why not?

Ed   Your mother has had to go into hospital.

Christopher   Can we visit her?

Ed   No.

Christopher   Why can't we?

Ed   She needs rest. She needs to be on her own.

Christopher   Is it a psychiatric hospital?

Ed   No. It's an ordinary hospital. She has a problem . . . a problem with her heart.

Christopher   I'll make her a get-well card.

If I make her a get-well card will you take it in for her tomorrow?

Scene Eight   School

Siobhan   How are you today, Christopher?

Christopher   I'm very well, thank you.

Siobhan   That's good.

Christopher   In the bus on the way to school we passed four red cars in a row.

Siobhan   Four?

Christopher   So today is a Good Day.

Siobhan   Great. I am glad.

Christopher   I've decided I am going to try and find out who killed Wellington because a Good Day is a day for projects and planning things.

Siobhan   Who's Wellington?

Christopher   Wellington is a dog that used to belong to my neighbour Mrs Shears who is our friend but he is dead now because somebody killed him by putting a garden fork through him. And I found him and then a policeman thought I'd killed him but I hadn't and then he tried to touch me so I hit him and then I had to go to the police station.

Siobhan   Gosh.

Christopher   And I am going to find out who really killed Wellington and make it a project. Even though Father told me not to.

Siobhan   Did he?

Christopher   Yes.

Siobhan   I see.

Christopher   I don't always do what I'm told.

Siobhan   Why?

Christopher   Because when people tell you what to do it is usually confusing and does not make sense. For example people often say 'Be quiet' but they don't tell you how long to be quiet for.

Siobhan   No. Why did your father tell you not to try to find out who killed Wellington?

Christopher   I don't know.

Siobhan   If your father's told you not to do something maybe you shouldn't do it.

Christopher   Mmm.

Siobhan   Well, we're meant to be writing stories today, so why don't you write about what happened to Wellington ?

Christopher   OK I will.

Scene Nine   Home

Ed   Christopher, I'm sorry, your mother's died.

She's had a heart attack.

It wasn't expected.

Christopher   What kind of heart attack?

Ed   I don't know what kind of heart attack. Now isn't the moment, Christopher, to be asking questions like that.

Christopher   It was probably an aneurysm.

Ed   I'm sorry, Christopher, I'm really sorry.

Scene Ten   School

Christopher   Reverend Peters, where is heaven?

Reverend Peters   I'm sorry, Christopher?

Christopher   In our universe whereabouts is it exactly?

Reverend Peters   It's not in our universe. It's another kind of place altogether.

Christopher   There isn't anything outside our universe, Reverend Peters. There isn't another kind of place altogether. Except there might be if you go through a black hole. But a black hole is what is called a singularity which means it's impossible to find out what is on the other side because the gravity of a black hole is so big that even electromagnetic waves like light can't get out of it, and electromagnetic waves are how we get information about things which are far away. And if heaven is on the other side of a black hole then dead people would have to be fired into space on a rocket to get there and they aren't or people would notice.

Reverend Peters *looks at him for a while before he responds.*

Reverend Peters   Christopher, we should talk about this on another day when I have more time.

Scene Eleven   Street

Siobhan   The next day was Saturday and there is not much to do on a Saturday unless Father takes me out somewhere on an outing to the boating lake or to the garden centre, but on this Saturday England were playing Romania at football which meant that we weren't going to go on an outing because Father wanted to watch the match on the television. So I made a decision. I decided to do some more detection. I decided to go out on my own.

I do not like strangers. So talking to the other people in our street was brave. But if you are going to do detective work you have to be brave, so I had no choice.

Mr Thompson   Can I help you?

Christopher   Do you know who killed Wellington?

Mr Thompson   Who are you?

Christopher   I'm Christopher Boone from number 36 and I know you. You're Mr Thompson.

Mr Thompson   I'm Mr Thompson's brother.

Christopher   Do you know who killed Wellington?

Mr Thompson   Who the fuck is Wellington?

Christopher   Mrs Shears's dog. Mrs Shears is from number 39.

Mr Thompson   Someone killed her dog?

Christopher   With a fork.

Mr Thompson   Jesus Christ.

Christopher   A garden fork.

Mr Thompson   Oh.

Christopher   Do you know who killed him?

Mr Thompson   Look, son, do you really think you should be going round asking questions like this?

Christopher   Yes I do, because I want to find out who killed Wellington and I am writing a book about it.

Mr Thompson   Well I was in Colchester on Thursday so you're asking the wrong bloke.

Christopher   Thank you for helping me with my investigation.

Do you know who killed Wellington?

Mr Wise   Bloody hell. Policemen really are getting younger aren't they?

He laughs. **Christopher** *walks away.*

Christopher   2 3 5 7 11 13 17 19 23 29 31 37 41 43 47 53 59 61 67.

Do you know anything about Wellington getting killed?

Mrs Alexander   I heard about it yesterday. Dreadful. Dreadful.

Christopher   Do you know who killed him?

Mrs Alexander   No, I don't.

Christopher   Somebody must know because the person who killed Wellington knows that they killed Wellington. Unless they were a mad person and didn't know what they were doing. Or unless they had senile dementia.

Mrs Alexander   You're Christopher, aren't you?

Christopher   Yes. I live at number 36.

Mrs Alexander   We haven't talked before, have we?

Christopher   No. I don't talk to strangers. But I'm doing detective work.

Mrs Alexander   I see you every day, going to school on your school bus. When I'm walking my dog. It's very nice of you to come and say hello. Even if it's only because you're doing detective work.

Christopher   Thank you.

Mrs Alexander   I have a grandson your age.

Christopher   My age is fifteen years and three months and three days.

Mrs Alexander   Well, almost your age. You don't have a dog, do you?

Christopher   No.

Mrs Alexander   You'd probably like a dog, wouldn't you?

Christopher   I have a rat.

Mrs Alexander   A rat?

Christopher   He's called Toby.

Mrs Alexander   Oh.

Christopher   Most people don't like rats because they think they carry diseases like bubonic plague. But that's only because they lived in sewers and stowed away on ships coming from foreign countries where there were strange diseases. But rats are very clean.

Mrs Alexander   Do you want to come in for tea?

Christopher   I don't go into other people's houses.

Mrs Alexander   Well, maybe I could bring some tea out here. Do you like lemon squash?

Christopher   I only like orange squash.

Mrs Alexander   Luckily I have some of that as well. And what about Battenberg?

Christopher   I don't know because I don't know what Battenberg is.

Mrs Alexander   It's a kind of cake. It has marzipan icing round the edge.

Christopher   Is it a long cake with a square cross-section that can be divided into equally sized, alternately coloured squares?

Mrs Alexander   Yes, I think you could probably describe it like that.

Christopher   I think I'd like the pink squares but not the yellow squares because I don't like yellow. And I don't know what marzipan is so I don't know whether I'll like that.

Mrs Alexander   I'm afraid marzipan is yellow too. Perhaps I should bring out some biscuits instead. Do you like biscuits?

Christopher   Yes. Some sorts of biscuits.

Mrs Alexander   I'll get a selection.

She goes into her house.

He waits. Then before she gets back:

Scene Twelve   School

Siobhan   She moved very slowly because she was an old lady and she was inside the house for more than six minutes and I began to get nervous because I didn't know her well enough to know whether she was telling the truth about getting orange squash and Battenberg cake. And I thought she might be ringing the police and then I'd get into much more serious trouble because of the caution. So I walked away.

The company cheer, as if a goal has been scored.

Christopher   Why would you kill a dog?

Siobhan   I wouldn't.

Christopher   I think you would only kill a dog if a) you hated the dog or b) if you were a mad person or c) because you wanted to make Mrs Shears sad. I don't know anybody who hated Wellington so if it was a) it was probably a stranger. I don't know any mad people either, so if it was b) it was also probably a stranger.

Siobhan   Right.

Christopher   But most murders are committed by someone who is known to the victim. In fact, you are most likely to be murdered by a member of your own family on Christmas Day.

Siobhan   Is that a fact?

Christopher   Yes actually it is a fact. Wellington was therefore most likely to have been killed by someone known to him. I only know one person who doesn't like Mrs Shears and that is Mr Shears who divorced Mrs Shears and left her to live somewhere else and who knew Wellington very well indeed. This means that Mr Shears is my Prime Suspect.

Siobhan   Christopher.

Christopher   I am going to find out more about Mr Shears.

Scene Thirteen   School Office

Mrs Gascoyne   Mr Boone, nobody has ever taken an A Level in the school before.

Ed   He can be the first then.

Mrs Gascoyne   I don't know if we have the facilities in the school to allow him to do that.

Ed   Then get the facilities.

Mrs Gascoyne   I can't treat Christopher differently to any other student.

Ed   Why not?

Mrs Gascoyne   Because then everybody would want to be treated differently.

Ed   So?

Mrs Gascoyne   It would set a precedent. Christopher can always do his A Levels later. When he's eighteen.

Ed   Christopher is getting a crap enough deal already, don't you think, without you shitting on him from a great height as well. Jesus, this is the one thing he's really good at.

Mrs Gascoyne   We should talk about this later. Maybe on our own.

Ed   Are there things which you're too embarrassed to say to me in front of Christopher?

Mrs Gascoyne   No. It's not that.

Ed   Say them now then.

Mrs Gascoyne   If Christopher sits an A Level then he would have to have a member of staff looking after him on his own in a separate room.

Ed   I'll pay for it. They can do it after school. Here. Fifty quid. Is that enough?

Mrs Gascoyne   Mr Boone.

Ed   I'm not going to take no for an answer.

He turns to **Christopher**.

Scene Fourteen   Home

Ed   Where have you been?

Christopher   I have been out.

Ed   I have just had a phone call from Mrs Shears. What the hell were you doing poking round her garden?

Christopher   I was doing detective work trying to figure out who killed Wellington.

Ed   How many times do I have to tell you, Christopher? I told you to keep your nose out of other people's business.

Christopher   I think Mr Shears probably killed Wellington.

Ed (*shouts*)   I will not have that man's name mentioned in my house.

Beat.

Everybody on stage pauses to look at **Ed** *and* **Christopher**.

Christopher   Why not?

Ed   That man is evil.

Christopher   Does that mean he might have killed Wellington?

Ed   OK, Christopher. I am going to say this for the last and final time. I will not tell you again. Look at me when I'm talking to you, for God's sake. Look at me. You are not to go asking Mrs Shears who killed that bloody dog. You are not to go asking anyone who killed that bloody dog. You are not to go trespassing on other people's gardens. You are to stop this ridiculous bloody detective game right now. I am going to make you promise me, Christopher. And you know what it means when I make you promise.

Scene Fifteen   Home

Siobhan   I think I would make a very good astronaut.

Ed   Yes, mate. You probably would.

Siobhan   To be a good astronaut you have to be intelligent and I'm intelligent. You also have to understand how machines work and I'm good at understanding how machines work.

Christopher   You also have to be someone who would like being on their own in a tiny spacecraft thousands and thousands of miles away from the surface of the earth and not panic or get claustrophobia or homesick or insane. And I really like little spaces so long as there is no one else in them with me.

Ed   I noticed.

Siobhan   Sometimes when I want to be on my own I get into the airing cupboard and slide in beside the boiler and pull the door closed behind me and sit there and think for hours and it makes me feel very calm.

Christopher   So I would have to be an astronaut on my own or have my own part of the spacecraft that no one else could come into. And also there are no yellow things or brown things in a spacecraft so that would be OK, too.

And I would have to talk to other people from mission control, but we would do that through a radio link-up and a TV monitor so it wouldn't be like real people who are strangers but it would be like playing a computer game.

Ed   Which you like.

Christopher   Also I wouldn't be homesick at all because I'd be surrounded by lots of things I like, which are machines and computers and outer space. And I would be able to look out of a little window in the spacecraft and know that there was no one else near me for thousands and thousands –

Ed   Christopher.

Christopher   What?

Ed   Could you please, just, give it a bit of a break, mate. Please.

Siobhan   And know that there was no one else near me for thousands and thousands of miles which is what I sometimes pretend at night in the summer when I go and lie on the lawn and look up at the sky and I put my hands round the sides of my face so that I can't see the fence and the chimney and the washing line and I can pretend I'm in space.

And all I could see would be stars. And stars are the places where the molecules that life is made of were constructed billions of years ago. For example, all the iron in your blood, which stops you being anaemic, was made in a star.

And I would like it if I could take Toby with me into space, and that might be allowed because they sometimes do take animals into space for experiments, so if I could think of a good experiment you could do with a rat that didn't hurt the rat, I could make them let me take Toby.

But if they didn't let me I would still go because it would be a Dream Come True.

Scene Sixteen   School

Christopher   Father said.

Siobhan   I see, that's a pity.

Christopher   So the book is finished.

Siobhan   Well, Christopher, if your father said he wanted you to stop then I think he probably has a good reason and I think you should stop. But you can still be very proud because what you've written so far is just, well it's great.

Christopher   It's not a proper book.

Siobhan   Why not?

Christopher   It doesn't have a proper ending. I never found out who killed Wellington. So the murderer is still At Large.

Siobhan   Not all murders are solved. Not all murderers are caught.

Christopher   Father said I was never to mention Mr Shears's name in our house again and that he was an evil man and maybe that meant he was the person who killed Wellington.

Siobhan   I think you should do what your father tells you to do.

Scene Seventeen   The Street

Mrs Alexander   What happened to you the other day? I came out again and you'd gone. I had to eat all the biscuits myself. I was looking forward to our little chat.

Christopher   I don't do chatting. I don't like it.

Mrs Alexander   No, I don't suppose you do. Do you like computers?

Christopher   Yes, I like computers. I have a computer in my room.

Mrs Alexander   I know. I can see you sitting at your computer in your bedroom sometimes when I look across the street.

Christopher   And I like maths and looking after Toby. And I also like outer space and I like being on my own.

Mrs Alexander   I bet you're very good at maths, aren't you?

Christopher   I am. I'm going to do A-Level Maths next month. And I'm going to get an A.

Mrs Alexander   Really? A-Level maths?

Christopher   I'm the first person to take an A Level from my school because it's a special school. All the other children at my school are stupid. Except I'm not meant to call them that, even though that is what they are.

Mrs Alexander   Well, I am very impressed. And I hope you do get an A.

Christopher   I will. Do you know Mr Shears?

Mrs Alexander   Not really, no. I mean I knew him well enough to say hello but I didn't know much about him. I think he worked in the National Westminster bank in town.

Christopher   Father said that he is an evil man. Do you know why he said that?

Mrs Alexander   Perhaps it would be best not to talk about these things, Christopher.

Christopher   Why not?

Mrs Alexander   Because maybe your father is right and you shouldn't go round asking questions about this.

Christopher   Why?

Mrs Alexander   Because obviously he is going to find it quite upsetting.

Christopher   Why is he going to find it quite upsetting?

Mrs Alexander   I think you know why your father doesn't like Mr Shears very much.

Christopher   Did Mr Shears kill Mother?

Mrs Alexander   Kill her?

Christopher   Yes. Did he kill Mother?

Mrs Alexander   No. No. Of course he didn't kill your mother.

Christopher   But did he give her stress so that she died of a heart attack?

Mrs Alexander   I honestly don't know what you're talking about, Christopher.

Christopher   Or did he hurt her so that she had to go into hospital?

Mrs Alexander   Did she have to go into hospital?

Christopher   Yes. And it wasn't very serious at first but she had a heart attack when she was in hospital.

Mrs Alexander   Oh my goodness.

Christopher   And she died.

Mrs Alexander   Oh my goodness. Oh, Christopher, I am so, so sorry. I never realised.

Christopher   Why did you say 'I think you know why your father doesn't like Mr Shears very much'?

Mrs Alexander   Oh dear, dear, dear. Christopher, look, perhaps we should take a little walk in the park together. This is not the place to be talking about this kind of thing.

Scene Eighteen   Park

Mrs Alexander   I am going to say something to you and you must promise not to tell your father that I told you this.

Christopher   Why?

Mrs Alexander   Christopher, please, just trust me.

Christopher   I promise.

Mrs Alexander   Your mother before she died was very good friends with Mr Shears.

Christopher   I know.

Mrs Alexander   No, Christopher, I'm not sure that you do. I mean that they were very good friends. Very, very good friends.

Christopher   Do you mean they were doing sex?

Mrs Alexander   Yes, Christopher. That is what I mean.

I'm sorry, Christopher. I really didn't mean to say anything that was going to upset you.

Christopher   Was that why Mr Shears left Mrs Shears, because he was doing sex with someone else when he was still married to Mrs Shears.

Mrs Alexander   Yes. I expect so.

Christopher   I think I should go now.

Mrs Alexander   Are you OK, Christopher?

Christopher   I can't be on my own with you because you are a stranger.

Mrs Alexander   I'm not a stranger, Christopher, I'm a friend.

Scene Nineteen   School

Ed *finds* **Christopher**'s *book on the kitchen table.*

Siobhan   Have you told your father about this?

Christopher   No.

Siobhan   Are you going to tell your father about this?

Christopher   No.

Ed *goes to the book.*

There is a tone.

He begins reading **Christopher**'s *book.*

Siobhan   Did it make you sad to find this out?

Christopher   Find what out?

Siobhan   Did it make you sad to find out that your mother and Mr Shears had an affair?

Christopher   No.

Siobhan   Are you telling the truth?

Christopher   Yes, I always tell the truth. It didn't make me feel sad because Mother is dead. So I would be feeling sad about something that isn't real and doesn't exist and that would be stupid.

Siobhan   What was your mother like?

Do you remember much about her?

Christopher   I remember the 20th of July 2010. I was nine years old. It was a Tuesday. We were on holiday in Cornwall. We were on the beach in a place called Polperro. Mother was wearing a pair of shorts made out of denim and a stripy blue swimming costume, and she was smoking menthol cigarettes, which were mint flavour. And she wasn't swimming. She was sunbathing on a towel, which had red and purple stripes, and she was reading a book by Georgette Heyer called *The Masqueraders*.

And then she finished sunbathing and went into the water and she said:

Judy   Bloody Nora, it's cold.

Scene Twenty   Beach

Christopher   'Bloody Nora, it's cold.' And she said I should come and swim too, but I didn't like swimming because I don't like taking my clothes off. And she said I should just roll my trousers up and walk into the water a little way. So I did. And Mother said:

Judy   Christopher! Look, it's lovely.

Christopher   And she jumped backwards and disappeared under the water and I thought a shark had eaten her and I screamed. And then she stood up out of the water and came over to where I was standing and held up her right hand and spread out her fingers like a fan.

Judy   Come on, Christopher, touch my hand. Come on now. Stop screaming. Touch my hand. Listen to me, Christopher. You can do it. It's OK, Christopher. It's OK. There aren't any sharks in Cornwall.

Ed   When we were inside the park Mrs Alexander stopped walking and said 'I am going to say something to you and you must promise not to tell your father that I told you this. Your mother before she died was very good friends with Mr Shears.'

Scene Twenty-One   Home

Ed   What is this?

Christopher *looks at* **Ed**.

Christopher   It's a book I'm writing.

Ed   Is this true? Did you speak to Mrs Alexander?

Christopher   Yes.

Ed   Jesus, Christopher, how stupid are you? What the fuck did I tell you, Christopher?

Christopher   Not to mention Mr Shears's name in our house. And not to go asking Mrs Shears or anyone about who killed that bloody dog. And not to go trespassing on other people's gardens. And to stop this ridiculous bloody detective game. Except I haven't done any of those things. I just asked Mrs Alexander about Mr Shears because I was doing chatting.

Ed   Don't give me that bollocks, you little shit. You knew exactly what you were bloody doing. I've read the book, remember. What else did I say, Christopher?

Christopher   I don't know.

Ed   Come on, Memory Man. Not to go round sticking your fucking nose into other people's business. And what do you do? You go around sticking your nose into other people's business. You go around raking up the past and sharing it with every Tom, Dick and Harry you bump into. What am I going to do with you, Christopher? What the fuck am I going to do with you?

Ed *throws* **Christopher**'s *book.*

Christopher   I was just chatting with Mrs Alexander. I wasn't doing investigating.

Ed   I ask you to do one thing for me, Christopher. One thing.

Christopher   I didn't want to talk to Mrs Alexander. It was Mrs Alexander who . . .

He screams.

Ed *and* **Christopher** *tussle.*

Ed *hits* **Christopher** *hard.*

Ed *stands above him.*

Ed   I need a drink.

He goes and picks up the book.

He leaves.

He comes back without the book.

Ed   I'm sorry I hit you. I didn't mean to.

I love you very much, Christopher. Don't ever forget that. I worry about you, because I don't want to see you getting into trouble, because I don't want you to get hurt.

Christopher   Where's my book?

Ed   Christopher, do you understand that I love you?

He holds his right hand up and spreads his fingers out in a fan.
Christopher *does the same with his left hand. They make their fingers and thumbs touch each other.*

Christopher   Is it in the dustbin at the front of the house?

Scene Twenty-Two   Map of House

Siobhan   The next day, when I got home from school, Father was still at work so I went outside and looked inside the dustbin.

But the book wasn't there.

I wondered if Father had put it into his van and driven to the tip and put it into one of the big bins there but I did not want that to be true because then I would never see it again. One other possibility was that Father had hidden my book somewhere in the house. So I decided to do some detecting and see if I could find it.

I started by looking in the kitchen.

Then I detected in the utility room.

Then I detected in the dining room.

Then I detected in the living room where I found the missing wheel from my Airfix Messerschmitt BF 109 G6 model under the sofa.

Then I went upstairs but I didn't do any detecting in my own room because I reasoned that Father wouldn't hide something from me in my own room unless he was being very clever and doing what is called a Double Bluff like in a real murder-mystery novel, so I decided to look in my own room only if I couldn't find the book anywhere else.

I detected in the bathroom, but the only place to look was in the airing cupboard and there was nothing in there.

Which meant the only room left to detect in was Father's bedroom.

I started by looking under the bed.

There were five shoes and a comb with lots of hair in it and a monkey wrench and a chocolate biscuits and a magazine called *Men Only* and a pair of underpants from Marks and Spencer's with a little bit of wee left in them and a Scooby Doo tie and a wooden spoon, but not my book. Then I looked in the drawers on either side of the dressing table. But these only contained aspirin and nail clippers and batteries and dental floss and tissues and a spare false tooth and a tampon but my book wasn't there either.

Then I looked in his clothes cupboard. In the bottom of the cupboard was a large plastic toolbox, which was full of tools for doing-it-yourself, but I could see these without opening the box because it was made of transparent grey plastic. Then I saw that there was another box underneath the toolbox.

The other box was an old cardboard box that is called a shirt box because people used to buy shirts in them.

He finds these things including, finally, the shirt box.

And when I opened the shirt box I saw my book was inside it.

He finds his book.

Then I heard Father's van pulling up outside the house and I knew that I had to think fast and be clever. I heard Father shutting the door of the van.

And that is when I saw the envelope.

It was an envelope addressed to me and it was lying under my book in the shirt box with some other envelopes. I picked it up.

He finds the envelope.

It had never been opened. It said:

Judy   Christopher Boone, 36 Randolph Street, Swindon, Wiltshire.

Siobhan   Then I noticed there were lots of envelopes and they were all addressed to me. And this was interesting and confusing.

And then I noticed how the words 'Christopher' and 'Swindon' were written. They were written like this.

Judy   Christopher. Swindon.

Siobhan   I only know three people who do little circles instead of dots over the letter i. And one of them is Siobhan. And one of them was Mr Loxley who used to teach at the school. And one of them was Mother.

Scene Twenty-Three   Back to Reality

Ed   Christopher?

Christopher   Hello.

Ed   So what have you been up to, young man?

Christopher   Today we did Life Skills with Siobhan. Which was Using Money and Public Transport. And I had tomato soup for lunch and three apples. And I practised some maths in the afternoon and we went for a walk in the park with Mrs Peters and collected leaves for making collages.

Ed   Excellent, excellent. What do you fancy for chow tonight?

Christopher   Baked beans and broccoli.

Ed   I think that can be very easily arranged.

I'm just going to put those shelves up in the living room if that's all right with you. I'll make a bit of a racket, I'm afraid, so if you want to watch television we're going to have to shift it upstairs.

Christopher   I'll go and be on my own in my room.

Ed   Good man.

Siobhan   So, I went in to my room. And when I was in the room I shut the door and took out the envelope. I opened the envelope. Inside there was a letter. And this was what was written in the letter.

Judy   451c Chapter Road, Willesden, London NW2 5NG. 0208 887 8907. Dear Christopher, I was looking through some old photos last night, which made me sad. Then I found a photo of you playing with the train set we bought for you a couple of Christmases ago. And that made me happy because it was one of the really good times we had together. Do you remember how you played with it all day and you refused to go to bed at night because you were still playing with it? We told you about train timetables and you made a train timetable and you made the train run on time. And there was a little wooden station, too, and we showed you how people who wanted to go on the train went to the station and bought a ticket and then got on a train. And you played with it for weeks and weeks and weeks. I liked remembering that a lot.

You haven't written to me yet, so I know that you are probably still angry with me. I'm sorry, Christopher. But I still love you. I hope you don't stay angry with me forever. And I'd love it if you were able to write me a letter.

I think about you all the time.

Lots of love,

Your Mum.

Siobhan   I was really confused. Mother had never written a letter to me before. And Mother had never lived in London.

I looked at the front of the envelope and I saw there was a postmark and there was a date on the postmark, the 16th of October 2015,

which meant that the letter was posted eighteen months after
Mother had died. When I started writing my book there was only
one mystery to solve. Now there were two. I decided not to think
about it anymore that night because I didn't have enough
information and could easily Leap to the Wrong Conclusions.

Scene Twenty-Four   Home

The next day **Christopher** *comes home from school.*

Ed   You're soaking.

Christopher   Yes.

Ed   Give me your coat, I'll hang it up.

How was school?

Christopher   It was good, thank you. Joseph Fleming took his
trousers off and went to the toilet all over the floor of the changing
room and started to eat it, but Mr Davis stopped him.

Ed   Good old Mr Davis, eh?

Christopher   Joseph eats everything.

Ed   Does he?

Christopher   He once ate one of the little blocks of blue
disinfectant which hang inside the toilets. And he once ate a £50
note from his mother's wallet. And he eats string and rubber bands
and tissues and writing paper and paints and plastic forks. Also he
bangs his chin and screams a lot.

Ed   I know how he feels. Christopher, I've got to go out.

Christopher   Why?

Ed   I've just had a call. There's a lady. Her cellar has flooded.
I've got to go out and fix it.

Christopher   Is it an emergency?

Ed   Yes, mate.

Christopher   It is raining very heavily.

Ed   It is.

Christopher   The rain looks like white sparks.

Ed   Christopher, if I go out, will you be OK?

Christopher   Yes I will because there's no one around because everybody's staying indoors.

Ed   Good. Good. Good. Good lad.

I'll have my mobile with me.

Christopher   Yes.

Ed   So you can call me if there's a problem.

Christopher   Yes.

Ed   Behave yourself, Christopher, yeah?

Christopher   Yeah.

Ed *exits.*

Siobhan   So I went into his bedroom and opened up the cupboard and lifted the toolbox off the top of the shirt box and opened the shirt box. I counted out the letters. There were forty-three of them. They were all addressed to me in the same handwriting. I took one and opened it. Inside was this letter.

As **Judy** *reads so* **Christopher** *begins to assemble his train set. His building becomes frantic. At times almost balletic.*

Judy   451c Chapter Road, London NW2 5NG. 0208 887 8907.

Dear Christopher. I said that I wanted to explain to you why I went away when I had the time to do it properly. Now I have lots of time. So I'm sitting on the sofa here with this letter and the radio on and I'm going to try and explain.

I was not a very good mother, Christopher. Maybe if things had been different, maybe if you'd been different, I might have been better at it. But that's just the way things turned out.

I'm not like your father. Your father is a much more patient person. He just gets on with things and if things upset him he doesn't let it show. But that's not the way I am.

Do you remember once when we were shopping in town together? And we went into Bentalls and it was really crowded and we had to get a Christmas present for Grandma? And you were frightened because of all the people in the shop. And you crouched down on the floor and put your hands over your ears and you were in the way of everyone so I got cross because I don't like shopping at Christmas either, and I told you to behave and I tried to pick you up and move you. But you shouted and you knocked those mixers off the shelf and there was a big crash. And everyone turned round to see what was going on and there were boxes and bits of string and bits of broken bowl on the floor and everyone was staring and I saw that you had wet yourself and I was so cross and I wanted to take you out of the shop but you wouldn't let me touch you and we just had to wait until you stopped screaming.

And I remember that night I just cried and cried and cried and your father was really nice about it at first and he made you supper and put you to bed and he said these things happen and it would be OK. But I said I couldn't take it anymore and eventually he got really cross and he told me I was being stupid and said I should pull myself together and I hit him, which was wrong, but I was so upset.

We had a lot of arguments like that.

And after a while we stopped talking to each other very much because we knew it would always end up in an argument. And I felt really lonely.

Siobhan   And that was when I started spending lots of time with Roger.

Judy   And that was when I started spending lots of time with Roger. And I know you might not understand any of this, but I wanted to try to explain so that you knew.

Siobhan   We had a lot in common. And then we realised that we were in love with one ano–

Judy   I said that I couldn't leave you and he was sad about that but he understood that you were really important to me.

Siobhan   And you started to shout and I got cross and I threw the food across the room. Which I know I shouldn't have done.

Judy   You grabbed the chopping board and you threw it and it hit my foot and broke my toes.

Siobhan   And afterwards at home your father and I had a huge argument.

Judy   And I couldn't walk properly for a month, do you remember, and your father had to look after you.

Siobhan   And I remember looking at the two of you and seeing you together and thinking how you were really different with him. Much calmer.

Judy   And it made me so sad because it was like you didn't need me at all.

Siobhan   And I think then I realised you and your father were probably better off if I wasn't living in the house.

Judy   And Roger asked me if I wanted to come with him.

Siobhan   And it broke my heart but eventually I decided it would be better for all of us if I went.

Judy   And so I said yes.

Siobhan   And I meant to say goodbye.

Judy   But when I rang your father he said I couldn't –

He was really angry. He said I couldn't –

Siobhan   He said I couldn't talk to you.

Judy   And I didn't know what to do.

Siobhan   He said I was being selfish and that I was never to set foot inside the house again.

Judy   And so I haven't.

Siobhan   I wonder if you can understand any of this. I know it will be difficult for you.

Judy   I thought what I was doing was the best for all of us. I hope it is.

Siobhan   Christopher, I never meant to hurt you.

Judy   I used to have dreams that everything would get better. Do you remember you used to say that you wanted to be an astronaut? Well I used to have dreams where you were an astronaut and you were on television and I thought that's my son. I wonder what it is that you want to be now. Has it changed? Are you still doing maths? I hope you are. Loads and loads of love, Mother.

Christopher *moves to the middle of the track. He crouches down. He rolls himself into a ball. He starts hitting his hands and his feet and his head against the floor as the letter continues.*

Christopher's *thrashing has exhausted him. He has been sick. He lies still for a while, wrapped in a ball.*

Ed   Christopher? Christopher? Christopher?

Christopher *doesn't respond.*

Ed   Christopher, what the hell are you doing? What are you? These are. Oh shit. Oh Christ.

Christopher *doesn't move or respond.*

Ed *stops himself from crying.*

Ed   It was an accident.

Christopher *doesn't respond.*

Ed   I don't know what to say. I was in such a mess. I said she was in hospital because I didn't know how to explain, it was so complicated. And once I'd said that I couldn't change it. It just . . . It got out of control.

Christopher *doesn't respond.*

After a time **Ed** *approaches him.*

Very, very gently he touches his shoulder. **Christopher** *doesn't respond.*

Ed   Oh, Jesus, Christopher. You've got sick all over your . . .

Let's sit you up and get your clothes off and get you into bed, OK? I'm going to have to touch you, but it's going to be all right.

He lifts **Christopher** *onto the side of the bed.* **Christopher** *doesn't resist or fight at all.* **Ed** *takes* **Christopher***'s jumper and shirt off.*

Scene Twenty-Five   Home

Ed   Look, maybe I shouldn't say this, but . . . I want you to know that you can trust me. Life is difficult, you know. It's bloody hard telling the truth all the time. But I want you to know that I'm trying. You have to know that I am going to tell you the truth from now on. About everything. Because . . . if you don't tell the truth now, then later on it hurts even more. So . . . I killed Wellington, Christopher. Just . . . let me explain. When your mum left . . . Eileen . . . Mrs Shears . . . she was very good to me. She helped me through a very difficult time. And I'm not sure I would have made it without her. Well, you know how she was round here most days. Popping over to see if we were OK. If we needed anything . . . I thought . . . Well . . . Christopher, I'm trying to keep this simple . . . I thought we were friends. And I guess I thought wrong. We argued, Christopher, and . . . She said some things I'm not going to say to you because they're not nice, but they hurt, but . . . I think she cared more for that bloody dog than for us. And maybe that's not so stupid, looking back. Maybe it's easier living on your own looking after some stupid mutt than sharing your life with other actual human beings. I mean, shit, buddy, we're not exactly low maintenance, are we? Anyway, we had this row. Well, quite a few rows to be honest. But after this particularly nasty little blow-out, she chucked me out of the house. And you know what that bloody dog was like. Nice as pie one moment, roll over, tickle its stomach. Sink its teeth into your leg the next. Anyway, we're yelling at each other and it's in the garden. So when she slams the door behind me the bugger's waiting for me. And . . . I know, I know. Maybe if I'd just given it a kick it would probably have backed off. But shit, Christopher, when the red mist comes down . . . Christ, you know what I'm talking about. I mean we're not that different me and you. And it was like everything I'd been bottling up for two years just . . .

I promise you, I never meant for it to turn out like this.

He holds his right hand up for **Christopher** *to touch.*

Christopher *ignores it.* **Ed** *stares at* **Christopher**.

Ed   OK. Look. Christopher. I'm sorry. Let's leave it for tonight, OK? I'm going to go downstairs and you get some sleep and we'll talk in the morning. It's going to be all right. Trust me.

He leaves. **Christopher** *groans. He starts counting.*

Christopher   2, 4, 8, 16, 32, 64, 128, 256, 512, 1024, 2048, 4096, 4096, 4096 –

Siobhan   Father had murdered Wellington. That meant he could murder me.

I had to get out of the house.

I made a decision. I did this by thinking of all the things I could do and deciding whether they were the right decision or not.

Ed   Stay home.

Siobhan   I decided I couldn't stay home anymore.

Ed   Christopher, please.

Christopher   No, because I can't live in the house with you anymore because it is dangerous.

I can't go and live with you because you can't look after me when school's closed.

Siobhan   I could try and –

Christopher   No, because you're a teacher.

Siobhan   Yes.

Christopher   Not a friend or a member of my family.

Uncle Terry   You could go and live with your Uncle Terry.

Christopher   You live in Sunderland. I don't know how to get to Sunderland.

Uncle Terry   Get a train. Get the train from Swindon.

Christopher   Also you smoke cigarettes. And you stroke my hair. You're not a friend either.

Mrs Alexander   I think I am a friend.

Christopher   No. And I can't stay overnight in your house or use your toilet because you've used it and you're a stranger.

Mrs Alexander   I'm not really a stranger, Christopher.

Christopher   Yes.

Judy   451c Chapter Road, London NW2 5NG.

451c Chapter Road, London NW2 5NG.

451c Chapter Road, London NW2 5NG.

Christopher *looks at* **Judy**.

Judy   451c Chapter Road.

Christopher   London NW2 5NG.

Scene Twenty-Six   School Room and School Hall

The company is on stage.

Siobhan   Christopher, I want to ask you something. Mrs Gascoyne wondered if we would like to do a play this year. She asked me to ask everybody if we'd like to make some kind of performance for the school. Everybody could join in and play a part in it.

Mrs Gascoyne   I think it would be a good thing for everybody to join in and play a part in it.

Siobhan   I was wondering if you'd like to make a play out of your book.

Christopher   No.

Siobhan   I think it could be really good fun, Christopher.

Mrs Gascoyne   I think it could be really good fun.

Christopher   No. It's a book and it's for me and not everybody, just for me.

Siobhan   I know that, but I think a lot of people would be interested in what would happen if people took your book and started acting bits out of it.

Christopher   No. I don't like acting because it is pretending that something is real when it is not really real at all so it is like a kind of lie.

Siobhan   But people like stories. Some people find things which are kind of true in things which are made up. You like your Sherlock Holmes stories and you know Sherlock Holmes isn't a real person, don't you?

I would help you if you were worried about that.

Christopher   No.

Reverend Peters   I think I'd rather like to take the part of a policeman.

Christopher   You're too old to be a policeman.

Ed (*shouting*)   Christopher. Christopher.

Company move into the space and watch **Ed**.

Christopher *hides.*

Nobody gives **Ed** *a clue as to where* **Christopher** *is. After a while he gives up.*

Then **Christopher** *comes out.*

He sees his dad's credit card on the floor. He stares at it, frozen in his tracks.

He approaches the card. He takes it, puts it in his pocket.

Voice Three   3558.

Voice Two   3558.

Voice One   3558.

Voice Six   3558.

Christopher   3558.

He leaves the house.

I knew that the train station was somewhere near. And if something is nearby you can find it by moving in a spiral, walking clockwise and taking every right turn until you come back to a road you've already walked on, then taking the next left, then taking every right turn and so on, and so on, and that was how I found the station.

Scene Twenty-Seven   Swindon Train Station

The voices here are pre-recorded.

Voice One   Customers seeking access to the car park please use assistance phone opposite, right of the ticket office.

Voice Two   Warning CCTV in operation.

Voice Three   Great Western.

Voice Five   Cold beers and lagers.

Voice Two   CAUTION WET FLOOR.

Voice Four   Your 50p will keep a premature baby alive for 1.8 seconds.

Voice Three   Transforming travel.

Voice Five   Refreshingly Different.

Voice One   It's delicious, it's creamy and it's only £1.30, Hot Choc Deluxe.

Voice Two   0870 777 7676.

Voice Four   The Lemon Tree.

Voice One   No Smoking.

Voice Two   Fine teas.

Voice Five   Automatic Fire Door Keep Clear.

Voice Two   Air Conditioned.

Voice Three   Reserved Parking.

Voice Four   Open As Usual This Way.

Voice Three   No Smoking.

Voice Five   No alcohol.

Voice Three   Dogs must be carried.

Voice One   RVP.

Voice Three   Dogs must be carried.

Voice One   LFB.

Voice Four   A Perfect Blend.

Voice Two   Royal Mail.

Voice Four   Mon–Fri 7 am–7 pm.

Voice Three   Dogs must be carried at all times.

Station Policeman   Hello, are you all right, young man?

Christopher   You're too old.

Station Policeman   Are you all right, young man?

Christopher   No.

Station Policeman　You're looking a bit worse for wear. The lady at the café says that when she tried talking to you, you were in a complete trance. What's your name?

Christopher　Christopher Boone.

Station Policeman　Where do you live?

Christopher　36 Randolph Street.

Station Policeman　What are you doing here?

Christopher　I needed to sit down and be quiet and think.

Station Policeman　OK, let's keep it simple. What are you doing at the railway station?

Christopher　I'm going to see Mother.

Station Policeman　Mother?

Christopher　Yes, Mother.

Station Policeman　When's your train?

Christopher　I don't know. She lives in London. I don't know when there's a train to London.

Station Policeman　So, you don't live with your mother?

Christopher　No. But I'm going to.

Station Policeman　So where does your mother live.

Christopher　In London.

Station Policeman　Yes, but where in London.

Christopher　451c Chapter Road, London NW2 5NG.

Station Policeman　Have you got a ticket?

Christopher　No.

Station Policeman　So how precisely were you going to get to London then?

Christopher　I have a cashpoint card.

Station Policeman   Is this your card?

Christopher   No, it's Father's.

Station Policeman   Father's.

Christopher   Yes, Father's.

Station Policeman   OK.

Christopher   He told me the number. It's 3558.

Station Policeman   Shhh. Why don't you and I take a stroll to the cash machine, eh?

Voice One   Please Insert Your Card.

Voice One   Enter Your Personal Number.

Station Policeman   You lead the way.

Christopher   Where?

Station Policeman   Back by the ticket office.

Voice One   Please Enter Amount. Ten Pounds. Twenty pounds. Fifty pounds. One Hundred Pounds.

Christopher   How much does it cost to get a ticket to London?

Station Policeman   About twenty quid.

Voice One   Please wait. Your transaction is being processed.

Christopher   Is that pounds?

Station Policeman   Christ alive. Yep. It's twenty pounds.

Voice One   Please take your card and wait for your cash.

Beat.

Christopher   Where do I get a ticket for the train from?

Station Policeman   In there.

Christopher   I want to go to London.

Man Behind Counter   If you don't mind.

Christopher   I want to go to London.

Man Behind Counter   Single or return?

Christopher   What does single or return mean?

Man Behind Counter   Do you want to go one way or do you want to come back?

Christopher   I want to stay there when I get there.

Man Behind Counter   For how long?

Christopher   Until I go to university.

Man Behind Counter   Single then. That'll be seventeen pounds.

Christopher   When is the train to London?

Man Behind Counter   Platform 1, five minutes.

Christopher   Where is Platform 1?

Man Behind Counter   Through the underpass and up the stairs. You'll see the signs.

Somebody bumps into **Christopher**. *He barks at them like a dog.*

Siobhan   Underpass means tunnel, Christopher.

In your head imagine a big red line across the floor. It starts at your feet and goes through the tunnel. And walk along the line. And count the rhythm in your head because that helps doesn't it? Like when you're doing music or when you're doing drumming. Left, right, left, right, left, right, left, right.

Christopher   Left, right, left, right, left, right, left, right, left, right.

Is this the train to London?

Scene Twenty-Eight   On Train

Station Policeman   Christopher. Caught you just in time. We've got your father at the police station. He's looking for you.

Christopher *tries to run. The* **Station Policeman** *grabs him.*
Christopher *screams. The* **Station Policeman** *lets go.*

Station Policeman   OK, let's not get over-excited here. I'm
going to take you back to the police station and you and me and
your dad can sit down and have a little chat about who's going
where.

Christopher   Have you arrested Father?

Station Policeman   Arrested him? What for?

Christopher   He killed a dog. With a garden fork. The dog was
called Wellington.

Station Policeman   Well, we can talk about that as well. Right
now, young man, I think you've done enough adventuring for
one day.

He reaches out to touch him. **Christopher** *screams.*

Station Policeman   Now listen, you little monkey.

The train begins to move.

Shitting fuck.

Christopher   Why are you swearing? Has the train started?

Station Policeman   Don't move.

Rob? Yeah, it's Nigel. I'm stuck here on the bloody train. Yeah.
Don't even . . . Look. It stops at Didcot Parkway. So if you can get
someone to meet me with a car . . . Cheers. Tell his old man we've
got him but it's going to take a while, OK? Great. Let's get
ourselves a seat.

Oh Christ, you're wetting yourself. For God's sake go to the
bloody toilet, will you?

Christopher   But I'm on a train.

Station Policeman   They do have toilets on trains, you know.

Christopher   Where is the toilet on the train?

Station Policeman   Through those doors there. But I'll be keeping an eye on you, you understand?

Christopher   No.

Station Policeman   Just go to the bloody toilet.

Christopher *stands.*

He walks down the corridor of the train. Shaking, closing his eyes, he pisses.

He tries to wash his hands but can't because there is no running water.

He spits on his hands to wash them. He rubs them dry with toilet paper.

Shaking, he leaves the toilet.

He goes to the luggage rack.

He climbs onto the shelf.

He hides himself.

He starts listing prime numbers to himself.

As he continues to count the **Station Policeman** *notices he's gone. The counting continues under the following exchanges.*

Christopher   2 3 5 7 11 13 17 19 23 29 31 37 41 43 47 53 59 61 67 71 73 79 83 89 97 101 103 107 109 113 127 131 137 139 149 151 157 163 167 173 179 181 191 193 197 199 211 223 227 229 233 239 241 251 257 263 269 271 277 281.

Station Policeman   Christopher? Christopher? Bloody hell.

He leaves. **Christopher** *stays where he is. Still counting. A* **Woman** *approaches him to take her bag.*

Woman on Train   Good God, you scared me. Can I just get my bag? I think someone's out there on the platform looking for you.

Christopher   I know.

Woman on Train   Well. It's your lookout.

She takes her bag. She leaves. **Christopher** *stays hidden behind the smaller pile of bags. Still counting. A* **Posh Woman** *approaches. She takes her bag.*

Posh Woman   You're touching my bag!

Christopher   Yes.

She leaves. **Christopher** *stays hidden behind the still smaller pile of bags. Still counting. Two* **Drunk Men** *approach to take their bags.*

Drunk One   Come and look at this, Barry. They've got, like, a train elf.

Drunk Two   Well, we have both been drinking.

Drunk One   We should nick him.

Drunk Two   He could be our elf mascot.

Drunk One   Come on, shift it, you daft twat.

A lady takes her bag; it is the wrong one. She realises.

Voice Six   Bollocks. That's not my bag.

Another lady runs to grab her bag; she is talking to someone on the platform.

Voice One   Coming. I'm coming, all right. Wait for me in the car park, then.

Both ladies take the correct bag and leave **Christopher** *alone. He stops counting. He lies still for a while.*

He looks around. For the first time he is alone on stage.

Christopher   I waited for nine more minutes but nobody else came past and the train was really quiet and it didn't move again so I realised that the train had stopped. And I knew that the last stop on the train was London.

So I got off the train.

He very tentatively gets down off the luggage rack and off the train.

Scene Twenty-Nine   Platform

Siobhan   Left, right, left, right, left, right . . .

Christopher   Left, right, left, right, left, right, left, right, left, right, left, right, left, right, left, right, left, right, left, right, left, right, left.

These **Voices** *are also recorded:*

Voice One   Sweet Pastries.

Voice Two   Heathrow Airport Check In Here.

Voice One   Bagel Factory.

Voice Five   EAT.

Voice Three   Excellence and taste.

Voice Four   YO! Sushi.

Voice One   Stationlink.

Voice Two   Buses.

Voice Five   WH Smith.

Voice Four   Mezzanine.

Voice One   Heathrow Express.

Voice Two   Clinique.

Voice Three   First Class Lounge.

Voice Four   Fuller's.

Voice Five   easyCar.co.

Voice Two   The Mad Bishop.

Voice Three   And Bear Public House.

Voice Four   Fuller's London Pride.

Voice One   Dixons.

Voice Two   Our Price.

Voice Three   Paddington Bear at Paddington Station.

Voice Five   Tickets.

Voice One   Taxis.

Voice Two   First Aid.

Voice Four   Eastbourne Terrace.

Voice Two   Way Out.

Voice One   Praed Street.

Voice Five   The Lawn.

Voice Three   Q Here Please.

Voice Four   Upper Crust.

Voice One   Sainsbury's.

Voice Five   Local information.

Voice Three   Great Western First.

Voice One   Position Closed.

Voice Two   Closed.

Voice Four   Position Closed.

Voice Three   Sock Shop.

Voice Four   Fast Ticket Point.

Voice Five   Millie's Cookies.

Voice One   Coffee.

Voice Two   Fergie to Stay at Manchester United.

Voice Three   Freshly Baked Cookies and Muffins.

Voice Two   Cold Drinks.

Voice Four   Penalty Fares.

Voice One   Warning.

Voice Three   Savoury Pastries.

Voice Four   Platform 14.

Voice Five   Burger King.

Voice Two   Fresh Filled.

Voice Three   The Reef Cafe Bar.

Voice Four   Business Travel.

Voice One   Special Edition.

Voice Two   Top 75 Albums.

Voice Five   *Evening Standard.*

As the chorus becomes more cacophonous **Christopher** *finds it more difficult to continue to walk. He stops. Rests his head against a box. Puts his hands over his ears. A* **Station Guard** *approaches him.*

Christopher *pulls out his Swiss Army knife.*

The **Station Guard** *backs away.*

Christopher *carries on.*

Christopher   Left, right, left, right, left, right, left, right.

He makes his hand into a telescope to limit his field of vision.

He approaches an information counter.

How do I get to 451c Chapter Road, London NW2 5NG?

Information   Where is that?

Christopher   It's 451c Chapter Road, London NW2 5NG. And sometimes you can write it 451c Chapter Road, Willesden, London NW2 5NG.

Information   Take the Tube to Willesden Junction. Or Willesden Green. Got to be near there somewhere.

Christopher   What is a Tube?

Ed   Don't do this, Christopher.

Christopher   Get away from me.

Ed   Christopher, you won't be able to.

Christopher   I'm doing really well.

Ed   You haven't got any money.

Christopher   I have. I stole your card.

Ed   You little shit. Where's your Swiss Army knife? Have you lost it?

Christopher   It's in my pocket.

Ed   Where's your red line gone? See? It keeps disappearing. There's no Jubilee Line. How are you going to get to Willesden Green?

Christopher   There's a Bakerloo Line. Look. I can take that to Willesden Junction.

Ed   Come back home.

Christopher   Swindon's not my home anymore. My home is 451c Chapter Road, London NW2 5NG.

Scene Thirty   Platform

The Tube line appears.

Ed   Stand behind the yellow line.

Christopher   I know.

Ed   The train will be very noisy.

Christopher   I know.

Ed   It'll really scare you.

Christopher   I know.

Ed   Try not to let it. Watch what the people do. Watch how they get on and off.

Christopher   Yes.

The company stand with **Christopher** *on the platform.*

Ed   Count the trains. Figure it out. Get the rhythm right.

Train coming. Train stopped. Doors open. Train going. Silence.

Train coming. Train stopped. Doors open. Train going. Silence.

Train coming. Train stopped. Doors open. Train going. Silence.

Train coming. Train stopped . . .

Christopher   . . . Doors open. Train going. Silence.

Train coming. Train stopped. Doors open. Train going. Silence.

Train coming. Train stopped. Doors open.

He is bundled onto the train.

Scene Thirty-One   Tube Train

Christopher   Is this train going to Willesden Junction?

The voices here are recorded.

Voice One   There are 53,963 holiday cottages in Scandinavia and Germany.

Voice Two   VITABIOTICS.

Christopher   Is this train going to Willesden Junction?

Voice Three   3435.

Voice Five   Penalty £20 fare if you fail to show a valid ticket for your entire journey.

Voice Four   Discover Gold, Then Bronze.

Christopher   Is this train going to Willesden Junction?

Voice One   TVIC.

Voice Three   EPBIC.

Voice Five   Obstructing the doors can be dangerous.

Voice Two   BRV.

Voice Three   Con. IC.

Christopher   Is this train going to Willesden Junction?

Voice Four   TALK TO THE WORLD.

Voice One   Warwick Avenue.

Maida Vale.

Kilburn Park.

Queen's Park.

Kensal Green.

Willesden Junction.

Scene Thirty-Two   Willesden Junction

Christopher *examines the A–Z. He opens it. He looks for Chapter Road.*

Christopher   Left. Right. Left. Right. Left. Right.

Left.

Right.

Left.

Right.

Left.

Right.

Left.

He closes the map. His voice quietens the more he talks. And as he talks he squats. And then huddles into a ball.

He sits silently, huddled for a while.

Scene Thirty-Three   Outside Judy's House

Judy *and* **Roger** *enter.*

Judy   I don't care whether you thought it was funny or not.

Roger   Judy, look, I'm sorry, OK.

Judy   Well, perhaps you should have thought about that before you made me look like a complete idiot.

Christopher *stands up.* **Judy** *sees him.*

The two look at one another.

Christopher   You weren't in so I waited for you.

Judy   Christopher.

Christopher   What?

Judy   Christopher.

She goes to hug him. He pushes her away so hard that he falls over.

Roger   What the hell is going on?

Judy   I'm so sorry, Christopher.

Judy *spreads her fingers.* **Christopher** *spreads his to touch hands with her.*

Roger   I suppose this means Ed's here.

Judy   Where's your father, Christopher?

Christopher   I think he's in Swindon.

Roger   Thank God for that.

Judy   But how did you get here?

Christopher   I came on the train.

Judy   Oh my God, Christopher. I didn't . . . I didn't think I'd ever . . . Why are you here on your own?

Christopher, you're soaking. Roger, don't just stand there.

Roger   Are you going to come in or are you going to stand out here all night?

Christopher   I'm going to live with you because Father killed Wellington with a garden fork.

Roger   Jumping Jack Christ.

Judy   Roger, please. Come on, Christopher. Let's go inside and get you dried off.

Roger   Come on then, soldier. You'll catch your death out here.

Christopher *doesn't move.*

Judy   You follow, Roger.

Christopher *does move. He gives Toby to* **Roger**.

Christopher   He's hungry. Have you got any food I can give him and some water?

Scene Thirty-Four   Inside Judy's House

Judy   Are you OK, Christopher?

Christopher   I'm tired.

Judy   I know, love. I can get you a blanket?

Christopher   No, don't. I've got a sleeping bag in my rucksack.

Judy   Will you let me help you get your coat off? You're very brave.

Christopher   Yes.

Judy   You never wrote to me.

Christopher   I know.

Judy   Why didn't you write to me, Christopher? I wrote you all those letters. I kept thinking something dreadful had happened or you'd moved away and I'd never find out where you were.

Christopher   Father said you were dead.

Judy   What?

Christopher   He said you went into hospital because you had something wrong with your heart. And then you had a heart attack and died.

Judy   Oh my God.

She starts to howl.

Christopher   Why are you doing that?

Judy   Oh, Christopher, I'm so sorry.

Christopher   What for?

Judy   Bastard. The bastard.

Christopher, let me hold your hand. Just for once. Just for me. Will you? I won't hold it hard.

Christopher   I don't like people holding my hand.

Judy   No. OK. That's OK.

Scene Thirty-Five   In Christopher's Bedroom at Judy's

London Policewoman   I need to speak to him.

Judy   He's been through enough today already.

London Policewoman   I know. But I still need to speak to him.

Christopher Boone. Please can you open the door.

Roger   Come on, Christopher.

Judy   Christopher, love. It's all right. Just open the door will you, sweetheart?

Christopher   Is she going to take me away?

Judy   No, Christopher, she isn't.

Christopher   Will you let her take me away?

Judy   No. I won't.

London Policewoman   Your father says you've run away. Is that right?

Christopher   Yes.

London Policewoman   Is this your mother?

Christopher   Yes.

London Policewoman   Why did you run away?

Christopher   Because Father killed Wellington who is a dog and so that meant that he could kill me.

London Policewoman   So I've been told. Do you want to go back to Swindon to your father or do you want to stay here?

Christopher   I want to stay here.

London Policewoman   And how do you feel about that?

Christopher   I want to stay here.

London Policewoman   Hang on, I'm asking your mother.

Judy   He told Christopher I was dead.

London Policewoman   OK. Let's . . . let's not get into an argument about who said what here. I just want to know whether . . .

Judy   Of course he can stay.

London Policewoman   Well, I think that probably settles it as far as I'm concerned.

Christopher   Are you going to take me back to Swindon?

London Policewoman   No.

If your husband turns up and causes any trouble, just give us a ring. Otherwise you're going to have to sort this out amongst yourselves.

Scene Thirty-Six   Middle of the Night, Corridor Outside Christopher's Bedroom

Ed   I'm talking to her whether you like it or not.

Judy   Roger. Don't. Just . . .

Roger   I'm not going to be spoken to like that in my own home.

Ed   I'll talk to you how I damn well like.

Judy   You have no right to be here.

Ed   He's my son in case you've forgotten.

Judy   What in God's name did you think you were playing at saying those things to him?

Ed   You were the one that bloody left.

Judy   So, you decided to just wipe me out of his life altogether?

Roger   Now let's just all calm down here, shall we?

Ed   Well, isn't that what you wanted?

Judy   I wrote to him every week.

Ed   What the fuck use is writing to him?

Roger   Whoa. Whoa. Whoa.

Ed   I cooked his meals. I cleaned his clothes. I looked after him every weekend; I looked after him when he was ill. I took him to the doctor. I worried myself sick every time he wandered off somewhere at night. I went to school every time he got into a fight. And you? What? You wrote him some fucking letters.

Christopher *gets up out of the sleeping bag.*

Judy   So you thought it was OK to tell him his mother was dead?

Roger   Now is not the time.

Christopher *finds his Swiss Army knife.*

Ed   I'm going to see him. And if you try to stop me . . .

He gets into **Christopher**'s *room.* **Christopher** *points his knife at him.*

Judy *comes in.*

Judy   It's OK, Christopher, I won't let him do anything. You're all right.

Ed   Christopher?

He squats down, completely exhausted.

Christopher *still points the knife at him.*

Ed   Christopher, I'm really, really sorry. About – . About – . About the letters. I never meant . . . I promise I will never do anything like that again.

He spreads his fingers and tries to get **Christopher** *to touch him.* **Christopher** *ignores him. He still holds his knife out. He groans.*

Ed   Shit. Christopher, please.

London Policewoman   Mr Boone.

Ed   What the fuck are you doing here? Did you call her?

London Policewoman   Mr Boone, come on, mate.

Ed   Don't you mate me. This is my son.

London Policewoman   I know. This can all be sorted out. Just come with me. Please.

Judy   Ed, you should go. He's frightened.

Ed   I'll be back.

Christopher. I'll be back. I promise you, Christopher. I promise you, lad.

Christopher *groans.*

London Policewoman *makes* **Ed** *leave.*

Roger *watches them both leave.*

Judy *and* **Christopher** *are left alone together.*

Judy   You go back to sleep now. Everything is going to be all right. I promise you.

They leave **Christopher** *in his room. He lies down. He settles.*

Scene Thirty-Seven   Judy's Kitchen

Immediately he has settled it is the next morning. **Roger** *and* **Judy** *give* **Christopher** *breakfast. He is overwhelmed by them.*

Roger   OK. He can stay for a few days.

Judy   He can stay as long as he needs to stay.

Roger   This flat is hardly big enough for two people, let alone three.

Judy   He can understand what you're saying, you know?

Roger   What's he going to do? There's no school for him to go to. We've both got jobs. It's bloody ridiculous.

He gives **Christopher** *a strawberry milkshake.*

Judy   Roger. That's enough. You can stay as long as you want to stay.

Christopher   It was Mother who gave me the milkshake.

They look at him.

It was Mother who gave me the milkshake not you.

Judy *picks the milkshake up.*

Christopher   You need to shout more loudly at him. Like you're really angry with him, not just being nice.

Judy *looks at him. Nods.*

Judy   OK.

She puts the milkshake down. She's much angrier.

Roger. That's enough. You can stay as long as you want to stay.

She looks at **Christopher**, *examining his response. Expecting more feedback.*

Christopher   I have to go back to Swindon.

They both look at him.

Judy   Christopher, you've only just got here.

Christopher   I have to go back because I have to sit my Maths A Level.

Judy   You're doing Maths A Level?

Christopher   Yes. I'm taking it on Wednesday and Thursday and Friday next week.

Judy   God. Christopher. That's really good.

Roger   Yeah.

Christopher   But I can't see Father. So I have to go back to Swindon with you . . .

Judy   I don't know whether that's going to be possible.

Christopher   But I have to go.

Judy   Let's talk about this some other time, OK?

Christopher   OK. But I have to go to Swindon.

He stands and leaves.

Judy   Christopher. Please.

Scene Thirty-Eight   Hampstead Heath

Judy   Would you like an ice lolly?

Christopher   Yes I would, please.

Judy   Would you like a strawberry one?

Christopher   Yes I would, please, because that's red. What's it called here?

Judy   It's called Hampstead Heath. I love it. You can see all over London.

Christopher   Where are all the planes going to?

Judy   Heathrow, I think.

Christopher, I rang Mrs Gascoyne.

I told her that you're going to take your Maths A Level next year.

Christopher *screams. He throws his ice lolly away.*

Judy   Christopher, please. Calm down. OK. OK, Christopher. Just calm down, love.

Christopher *screams and screams. He only stops because his chest hurts and he runs out of breath.*

Scene Thirty-Nine   Judy's Home

Roger *gives* **Christopher** *a radio and three children's books.*

Roger   Here we are. You wanted a radio. *100 Number Puzzles.* It's from the library. This one is called *The Origins of the Universe.* And this one is *Nuclear Power.*

Christopher   They're for children.

Roger   Well, it's nice to know my contribution is appreciated.

Scene Forty   Judy's Home

Christopher *picks up the radio. He leaves. He de-tunes it so that it is between two stations. He listens to the white noise. He turns the volume up very high.*

Some time.

Roger *watches him. He opens and drinks four cans of lager. He necks the lager in one go.*

He comes into **Christopher's** *room. He is very drunk.*

Roger   You think you're so clever, don't you? Don't you ever, ever think about other people for one second, eh? Well, I bet you're really pleased with yourself now, aren't you?

He grabs at **Christopher.** **Christopher** *rolls himself into a ball to hide.*

Judy *comes into the room. She grabs* **Roger.** *She pulls him away from* **Christopher.**

Christopher *is moaning still in his ball.*

Judy   Christopher, I'm sorry. I'm really, really sorry. I promise this will never happen again.

He remains in his ball.

He doesn't stop moaning.

Judy *and* **Roger** *leave.*

Eventually he calms.

Scene Forty-One   Judy's Home

Christopher   What time is it?

Judy   Shhh, it's four o'clock in the morning.

Christopher   What are you doing?

Judy   I'm packing some clothes.

Christopher   Where's Mr Shears?

Judy   He's asleep.

Come downstairs. Bring Toby. Get into the car.

Christopher   Into Mr Shears's car?

Judy   That's right.

Christopher   Are you stealing the car?

Judy   I'm just borrowing it.

Christopher   Where are we going?

Judy   We're going home.

Christopher   Do you mean home in Swindon?

Judy   Yes.

Christopher   Are we going back to Swindon so I can do my Maths A Level?

Judy   What?

Christopher   I'm meant to be doing my Maths A Level tomorrow.

Judy   We're going back to Swindon because if we stay in London any longer . . . someone is going to get hurt. And I don't necessarily mean you.

Now I need you to be quiet for a while.

Christopher   How long do you need me to be quiet for?

Judy   Jesus. Half an hour, Christopher. I need you to be quiet for half an hour.

Scene Forty-Two   Home

Ed   How the fuck did you get in here?

Judy   This is my house, too, in case you've forgotten.

Ed   Is your fancy man here as well?

Christopher *starts drumming on one of the boxes. He begins drumming on them. He drums and drums and drums.* **Ed** *and* **Judy** *talking inaudibly under the drumming.*

Judy   Christopher. Christopher.

He's gone. You don't need to panic.

Christopher   Where's he gone to?

Judy   He's gone to stay at his friend's house for a while.

Christopher   Is he going to be arrested? And go to prison?

Judy   What for?

Christopher   For killing Wellington.

Judy   I don't think so. I think he'll only get arrested if Mrs Shears presses charges.

Christopher   What's that?

Judy   It's when you tell the police to arrest somebody for little crimes. They only arrest people for little crimes if you ask them.

Christopher   Is killing Wellington a little crime?

Judy   Yes, love, it is.

In the next few weeks we're going to try and get a place of our own to live in.

Christopher   Can I still take my A Level?

Judy   You're not listening to me are you, Christopher?

Christopher   I am listening to you.

Judy   I told you. I rang your headmistress. I told her you were in London. I told her you'd do it next year.

Christopher   But I'm here now so I can take it.

Judy   I'm sorry, Christopher. I didn't know we'd be coming back. This isn't going to solve anything.

Scene Forty-Three   Street

Mrs Shears   You've got a fucking nerve.

Christopher   Where are we going?

Mrs Shears   Swanning round here as though nothing ever happened.

Judy   Ignore her, Christopher.

Mrs Shears   So he's finally dumped you too, has he?

Christopher   What is Mrs Shears doing?

Mrs Shears   You had it coming. Don't try and pretend that you didn't. Because you fucking did.

Christopher   Where are we going?

Judy   We're going to the school.

Scene Forty-Four   School

Siobhan   So you're Christopher's mother.

Judy   That's right. And you're . . .

Siobhan   I'm Siobhan. It's nice to meet you.

Judy   Yeah. Yes. Yes. It's nice to meet you too.

Siobhan   Hello, Christopher.

Christopher   Hello.

Siobhan   Are you OK?

Christopher   I'm tired.

Judy   He's a bit upset.

Siobhan   Because of the A Level, you said.

Judy   He won't eat. He won't sleep.

Siobhan   Yeah.

I spoke to Mrs Gascoyne after you called.

Judy   Right.

Siobhan   She still actually has your A-Level papers in the three sealed envelopes in her desk.

Mrs Gascoyne   I still actually have the A-Level papers in my desk.

Christopher   Does that mean I can still do my A Level?

Siobhan   I think so. We're going to call the Reverend Peters to make sure he can still come in this afternoon and be your invigilator. And Mrs Gascoyne is going to call the examination board to say that you're going to take the exam after all. I thought I should tell you now. So you could think about it.

Christopher   So I could think about what?

Siobhan   Is this what you want to do, Christopher? If you say you don't want to do it no one is going to be angry with you. And it won't be wrong or illegal or stupid. It will just be what you want and that will be fine.

Christopher   I want to do it.

Siobhan   OK.

How tired are you?

Christopher   Very.

Siobhan   How's your brain when you think about maths?

Chirstopher   I don't think it really works very well.

Siobhan   What's the logarithmic formula for the approximate number of prime numbers not greater than x?

Christopher   I can't think.

Scene Forty-Five   Exam Room

Reverend Peters *enters. He picks up one envelope. He opens it. He looks at it. He carefully places it face down on* **Christopher**'s *table.*

He goes to sit opposite him. He takes out a stopwatch.

Reverend Peters   So this is jolly exciting, eh, Christopher? Well I'm excited anyway. Now the exam is going to last for two hours Christopher, OK? First thing to do is to pop your name on the front. OK, young man, are you ready to roll? Turn over the paper please, Christopher. And begin.

Christopher *turns over the exam paper.*

He stares at it.

He can't understand any questions. He panics. His breathing becomes erratic. To calm himself he counts the cubes of cardinal numbers.

Christopher   1, 8, 27, 64, 125, 216, 343, 512, 729, 1000, 1331.

Reverend Peters   Are you all right, Christopher?

Christopher   I can't read the question.

Reverend Peters   What do you mean?

Christopher   I can't read the question.

Reverend Peters   Can you see the question?

Christopher   I can see the question but I can't read the question because when I look at the words they all seem confused and mixed up and the wrong way round to me.

Reverend Peters   Right.

Christopher   What does this question say?

Reverend Peters   Christopher, I'm afraid I can't help you like that. I'm not allowed to.

Christopher *groans.*

Siobhan   Christopher. Stop groaning. Get your breath. Count the cubes of the cardinal numbers again.

Christopher   1, 8, 27, 64, 125, 216, 343, 512, 729, 1000, 1331.

Siobhan   Now. Have another go.

He looks at the questions again.

Christopher   Show that a triangle with sides that can be written in the form n squared plus one, n squared minus one and two n (where n is greater than one) is right-angled.

Siobhan   You don't have to tell us.

Christopher   What?

Siobhan   You don't have to tell us how you solved it.

Christopher   But it's my favourite question.

Siobhan   Yes but it's not very interesting.

Christopher   I think it is.

Siobhan   People won't want to hear about the answer to a maths question in a play.

Look, why don't you tell it after the end of the play?

When you've finished you can do a bow and then people who want to can go back to class and if anybody wants to find out how you solved the maths question then they can stay and you can tell them at the end.

OK?

Christopher   OK.

He picks up his pencil.

He starts answering.

Scene Forty-Six   Home

Ed *enters.*

Judy *is behind him.*

Ed   Don't scream.

OK, Christopher. I'm not going to hurt you.

He crouches down by **Christopher**.

Ed   I wanted to ask you how the exam went.

Judy   Tell him, Christopher.

Please, Christopher.

Christopher   I don't know if I got all the questions right because I was very tired and I hadn't eaten any food so I couldn't think properly.

Ed *nods. There is some time.*

Ed   Thank you.

Christopher   What for?

Ed   Just . . . thank you. I'm very proud of you, Christopher. Very proud. I'm sure you did really well.

Scene Forty-Seven   School

Siobhan   How's your flat?

Christopher   It's not really a flat. It's a room. It's very small. The corridor's painted brown. Other people use the toilet. Mother has to clean the toilet before I can use it. Sometimes there are other people in there so I do wet myself. The room smells like socks and pine air freshener. And another bad thing that happened is that Toby died. Because he was two years and seven months old which is very old for a rat. I don't like waiting for my A-Level result.

Mother doesn't get back from work till 5.30. So I have to go to Father's house between 3.49 and 5.30 because I'm not allowed to be on my own. Mother said I didn't have a choice. I push the bed up against the door in case Father tries to come into the room. Sometimes he tries to talk to me through the door. I don't answer him. Sometimes he sits outside the door quietly for a long time.

Can I come and live in your house so that I'll have room to put all my things and I wouldn't have to share the toilet with strangers?

Siobhan   No, Christopher. You can't.

Christopher   Why can't I? Is it because I'm too noisy and sometimes I'm 'difficult to control'?

Siobhan   No. It's because I'm not your mother.

Christopher   No.

Siobhan   That's very important. Do you understand that?

Christopher   I don't know.

Scene Forty-Eight   Home

Ed *enters. He's holding a kitchen timer.*

Ed   Christopher, can I have a talk with you?

Christopher *turns away from* **Siobhan**.

Christopher   No. No. No. No. No. No you can't. No.

Judy   It's OK. I'll be here.

Christopher   I don't want to talk to Father.

Ed   I'll do you a deal. Five minutes, OK? That's all.

He sets the timer for five minutes. It starts ticking.

Christopher, look . . . Things can't go on like this. I don't know about you, but this . . . this just hurts too much, you being in the house and not talking to me. You have to learn to trust me . . . And I don't care how long it takes . . . if it's a minute one day and two minutes the next and three minutes the next and it takes years I don't care. Because this is important. This is more important than anything else. Let's call it . . . let's call it a project. A project we have to do together. And it will be difficult at first because . . . because it's a difficult project. But it will get better, I promise. And . . . I've got you a present. To show you that I really mean what I say. And to say sorry. And because . . . well you'll see what I mean.

He leaves.

He comes back with a box. It is importantly cardboard and different to the other boxes. There's a blanket in it. He puts his hands in the box. He takes out a little sandy-coloured Golden Retriever.

He's two months old.

Christopher, I would never ever do anything to hurt you.

The dog sits on **Christopher***'s lap.*

Judy   You won't be able to take him away with you, I'm afraid. The bedsit's too small. But your father's going to look after him here. And you can come and take him out for walks whenever you want.

Christopher   Does he have a name?

Ed   No. You can decide what to call him.

Christopher   Sandy. He's called Sandy.

The alarm goes off.

They look at each other.

Judy   We need to go now.

Ed   Yes.

Judy   We'll come back tomorrow and you can see him then.

Scene Forty-Nine   School

Siobhan   Christopher.

Christopher   Yes.

Siobhan   Here.

Christopher   What's this?

Siobhan   It's your result.

Christopher   Right.

Siobhan   You need to open it and read it.

Christopher   Right.

He does.

Siobhan   Well? What does it say?

Christopher   I got an A*.

Siobhan   Oh. Oh. That's just. That's terrific.

Christopher   Yes.

Siobhan   Aren't you happy?

Christopher   Yes. It's the best result.

Siobhan   I know it is. How's your dog?

Christopher   He's very well, thank you. I stayed last week at Father's because Mother got flu and he slept on my bed so he can bark in case anybody came into the room at night.

Siobhan   Right. How are you getting on with your father?

Christopher   He planted a vegetable patch in his garden. I helped him and Sandy watched. We planted carrots and peas and spinach and I'm going to pick them when they're ready. He bought me a book, which is called *Further Maths for A Level*. He told Mrs Gascoyne that I was going to take Further Maths next year. She said OK.

Mrs Gascoyne   OK.

Christopher   I'm going to pass it and get an A*. And then in two years I'll take A-Level Physics and get an A*. And then I'm going to go to university in another town. I can take Sandy and my books and my computer. I can live in a flat with a garden and a proper toilet. Then I will get a first-class honours degree. Then I will be a scientist. I can do these things.

Siobhan   I hope so.

Christopher   I can because I went to London on my own.

She looks at him.

I solved the mystery of Who Killed Wellington.

She looks at him.

I found my mother. I was brave.

Siobhan   You were.

Christopher   And I wrote a book.

Siobhan   I know. I read it. We turned it into a play.

Christopher   Yes. Does that mean I can do anything do you think?

Does that mean I can do anything, Siobhan?

Does that mean I can do anything?

The two look at each other for a while.

Lights black.

After the curtain call **Christopher** *returns to the stage. He gets the attention of anybody still in the audience. Even if it is just one person. He thanks them for staying.*

Using as much theatricality as we can throw at it, using music, lights, sound, lasers, the boxes, the train tracks, the rest of the company, the orchestra, the fucking ushers for Christ's sake, using dance, song, bells, whistles, the works, he proves by means of a counter-example that a triangle with sides that can be written in the form n *squared plus one,* n *squared minus one and two* n *(where* n *is greater than one) is right-angled.*

Maths Appendix

After the applause, lights down, smoke, **Christopher** *appears rising through the centre trap. There is very cool, electro music.*

Thank you very much for clapping and thank you very much for staying behind to listen to how I answered the question on my Maths A Level. Siobhan said it wouldn't be very interesting but I said it was.

I had two hours to answer nineteen questions – but I spent thirty-eight minutes doing moaning and groaning which meant I only had four minutes to answer this question.

A timer is projected – displaying 4.00.00

Show that a triangle with sides that can be written in the form n squared plus one, n squared minus one and two n (where n is bigger than 1) is right-angled.

And this is what I wrote.

He runs and starts the timer.

Start the clock.

A right-angled triangle is made using projection (or lasers if you have the money or holograms if you are in the future).

If a triangle is right-angled, one of its angles will be 90 degrees and will therefore follow Pythagoras' theorem.

Pythagoras said that a squared plus b squared equals c squared, to put it simply.

If you draw squares outside the three sides of a right-angled triangle then add up the area of the two smaller squares, this will be equal to the area of the larger square. This is only true if the triangle is right-angled.

The A-Level question is an algebraic formula for making right-angled triangles.

N squared plus one is the biggest number in this equation, which makes it the hypotenuse, which is the longest side of the triangle.

To find the area of a square you must multiply the length by the width.

So . . . the area of this square is

$2n \times 2n$.

Which equals $4n$ squared.

The area of this square is

(n squared minus 1) $\times$ (n squared minus 1).

Which equals n to the power of 4 minus $2n$ squared plus 1.

Now, if we add these two squares together . . .

This equals n to the power of 4 plus $2n$ squared plus 1.

NOW . . . . We need to find the area of the square on the hypotenuse which is:

(n squared plus 1) $\times$ (n squared plus 1).

Which equals n to the power of 4 plus $2n$ squared plus 1.

Which is THE SAME TERM!

So the area of the two small squares adds up to the area of the larger square.

So all my squares fit together to satisfy Pythagoras' theorem.

So the triangle is – RIGHT-ANGLED!

And that is how I got an A*.

Confetti.

He exits.

CPSIA information can be obtained
at www.ICGtesting.com
Printed in the USA
LVHW082024020620
657248LV00017B/650

9 781350 111530